What If...

Alicia Winget

Illustrations by
Caralyn Tignanelli

WestBow Press books may be ordered through booksellers or by contacting:

WestBow Press
A Division of Thomas Nelson
1663 Liberty Drive
Bloomington, IN 47403
www.westbowpress.com
1-(866) 928-1240

Because of the dynamic nature of the Internet, any web addresses or links contained in this book may have changed since publication and may no longer be valid. The views expressed in this work are solely those of the author and do not necessarily reflect the views of the publisher, and the publisher hereby disclaims any responsibility for them.

Any people depicted in stock imagery provided by Thinkstock are models, and such images are being used for illustrative purposes only.

Certain stock imagery © Thinkstock.

ISBN: 978-1-4497-8073-9 (sc)
ISBN: 978-1-4497-8074-6 (e)

Library of Congress Control Number: 2012924218

Printed in the United States of America

WestBow Press rev. date: 1/14/2013

WestBow
PRESS
A DIVISION OF THOMAS NELSON

What if,
while seeing the
power of wind,

Or of river flow,
no one imagined

Harnessing that strength;
using that strong air,

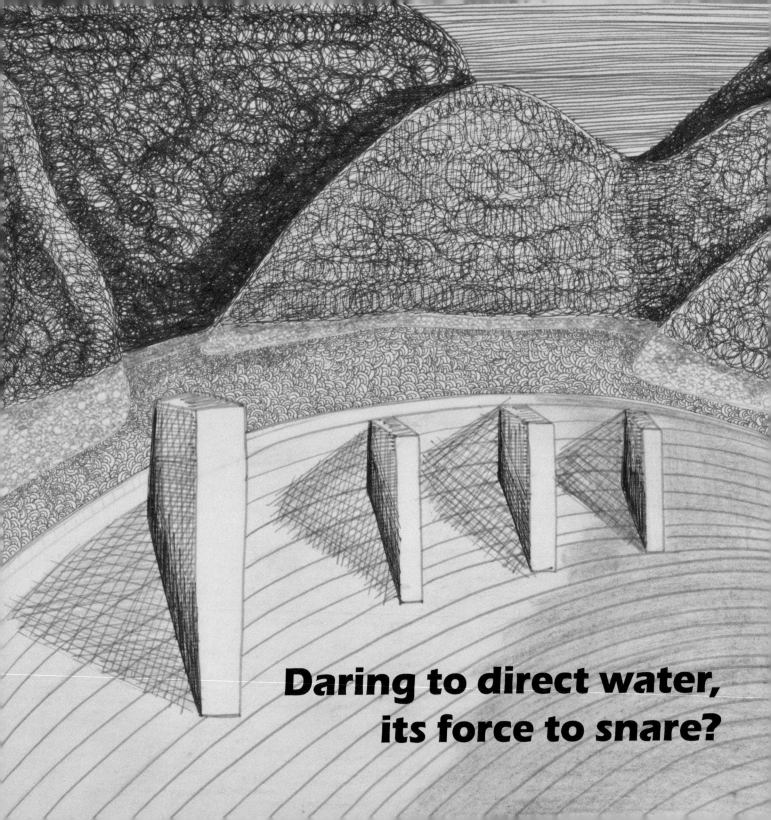

**Daring to direct water,
its force to snare?**

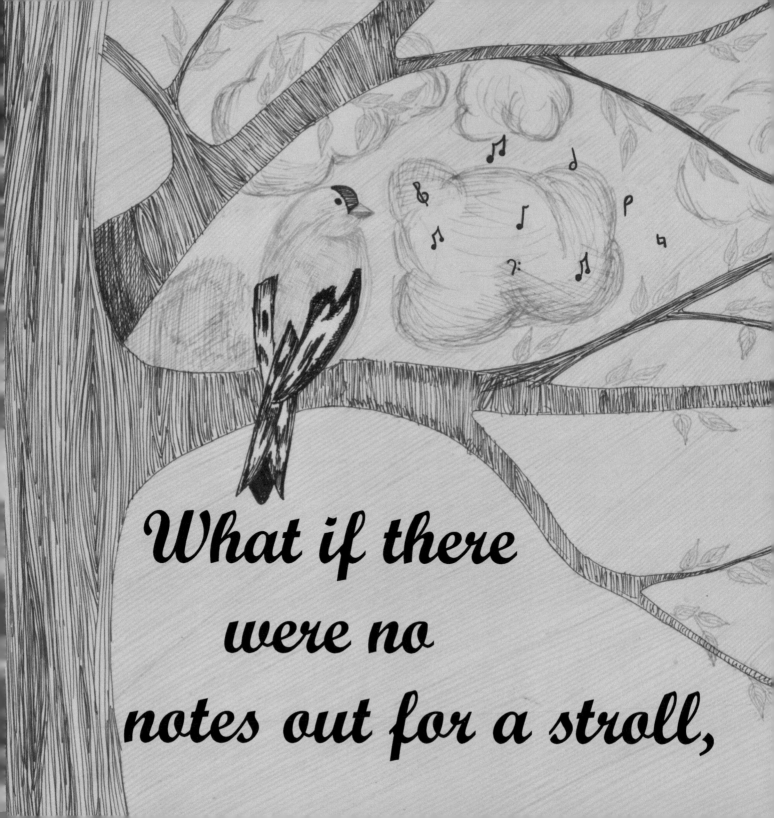

No lullabies hummed
to calm and console;

No haunting, beautiful
symphonic strains,

What if there were no

stories fantastic;

Once Upon A Time the lived

No one pursuing

projects scholastic,

Or penning works of intrigue, mystery?

What if no one recorded history?

What if no one brushed

impressionistic,

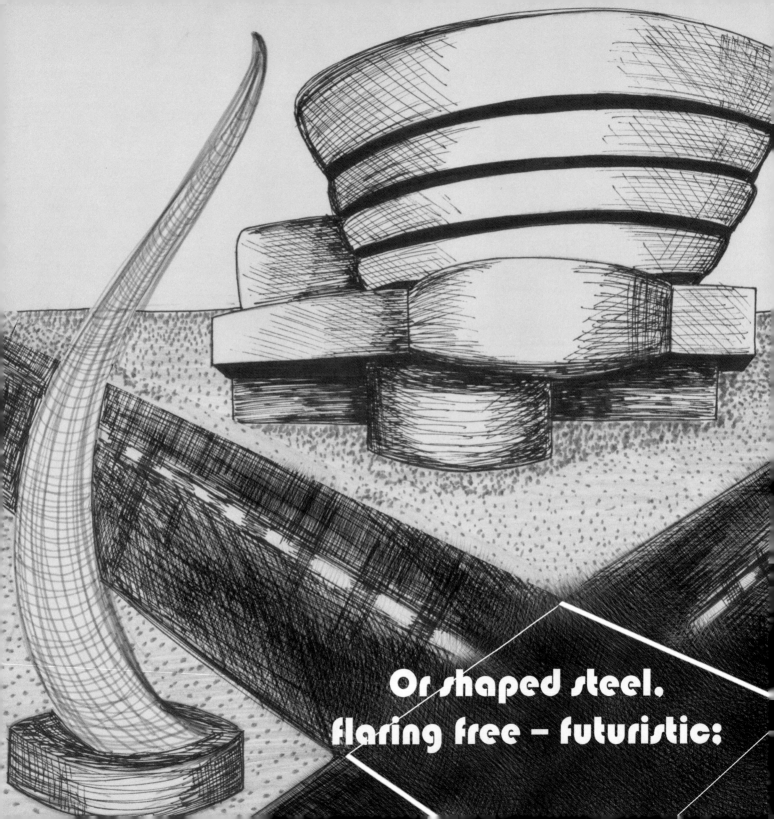

Or shaped steel,
flaring free — futuristic;

NO ONE PAINTED BIG, BROAD
AND BOLDLY BRIGHT,

Or water colored a soft, soothing sight?

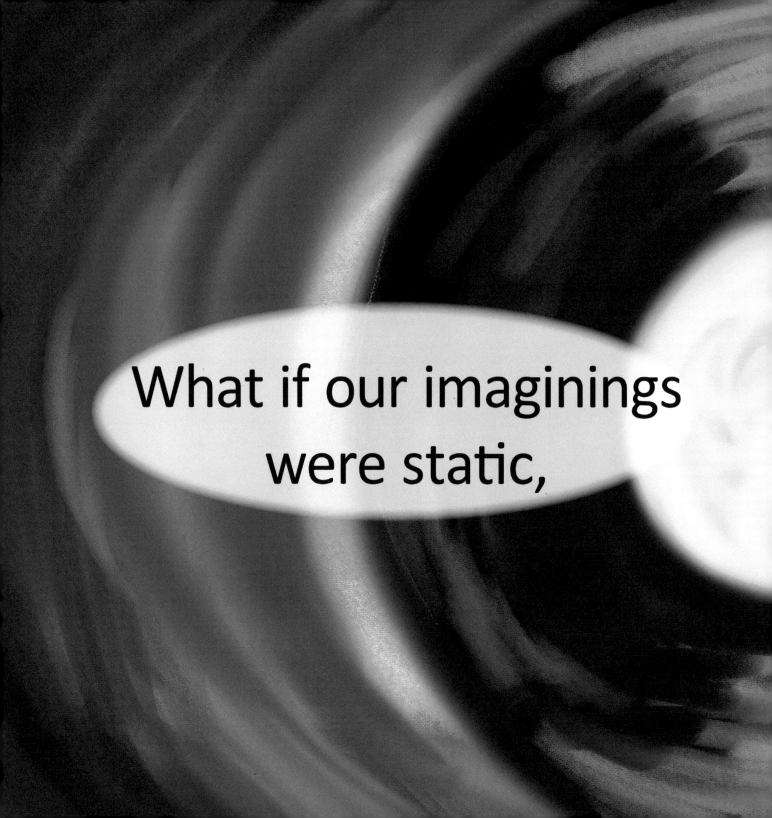

While eyeing the bird

in its swoop and glide,

Or watching the sea mammal breach and dive?

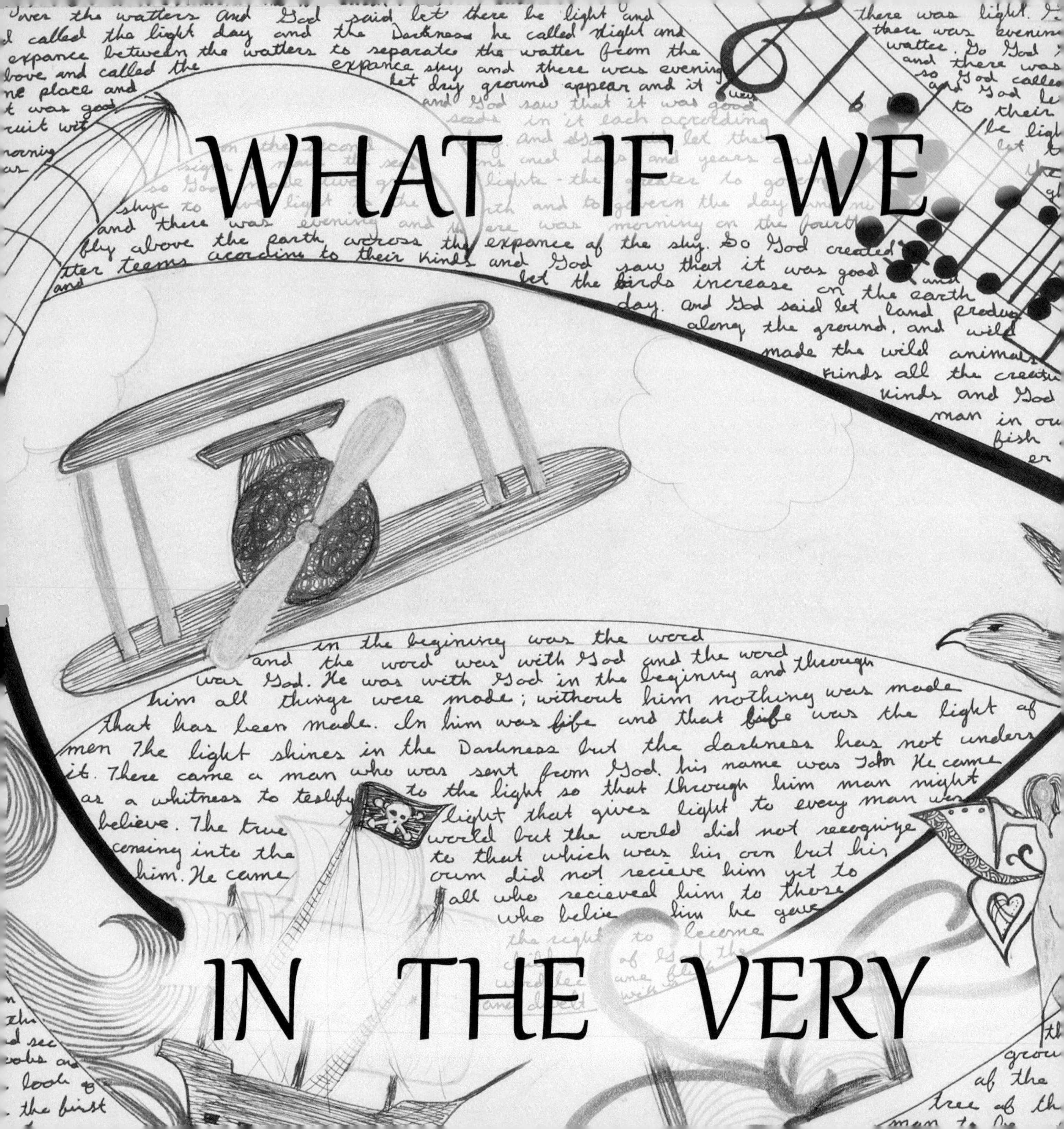
WHAT IF WE
IN THE VERY

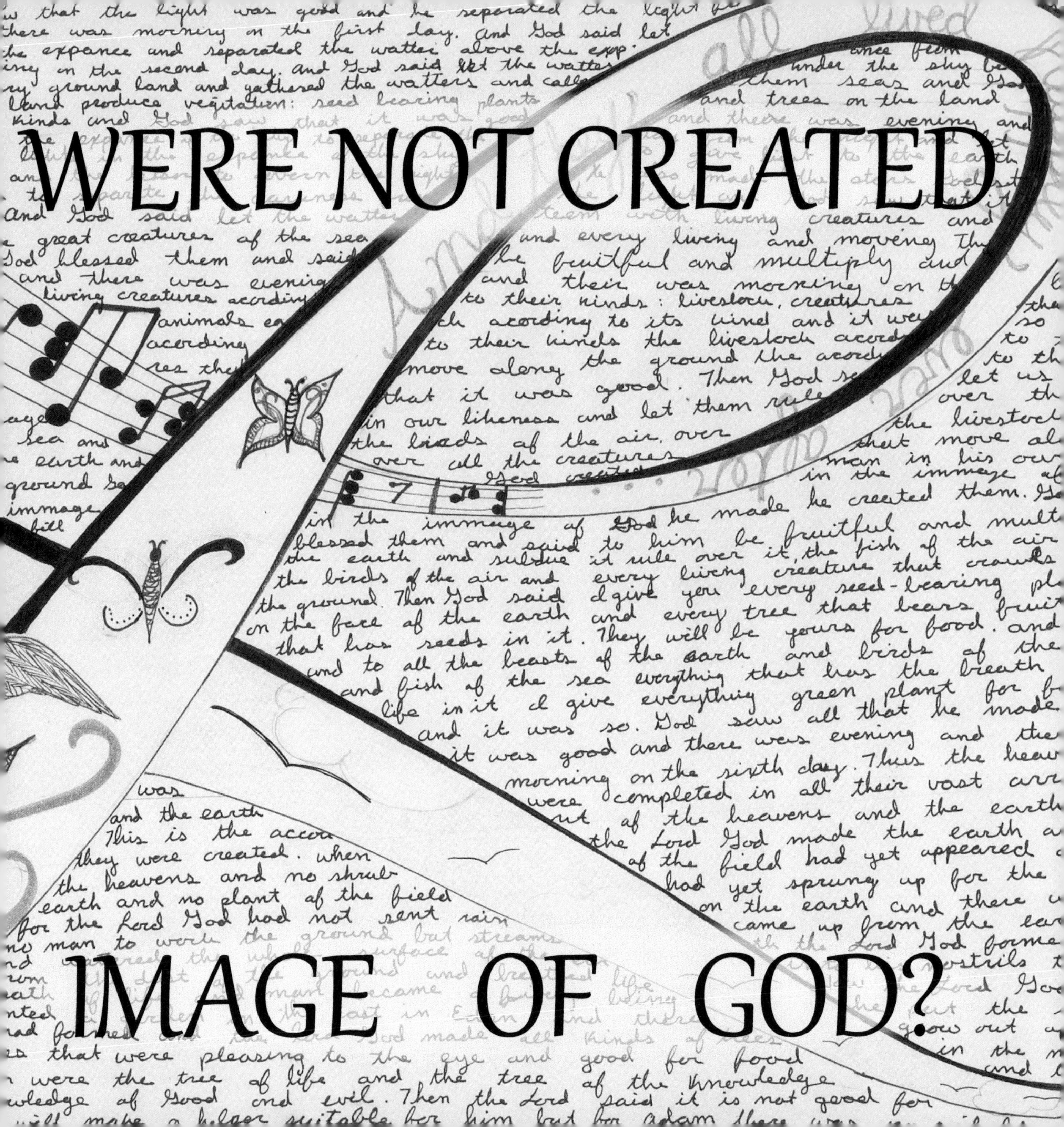

WERE NOT CREATED

IMAGE OF GOD?